Your Fre

I wanted to show my appreciation that you support my work so I've put together a free gift for you.

Slowcooker Essentials Cookbook
http://thezenfactory.com/ninja_master_free_book/

Just visit the link above to download it now.

I know you will love this gift.

Thanks!

Table of Content

Introduction

If you want to lose weight, or you simply want to start eating healthy foods; this book is exactly what you are looking for. By using the amazing Nutri Ninja Master Blender, you will be able to turn a bunch of ingredients into the best healthy smoothie that you will ever taste thanks to its sharp blades that slice the veggies and fruits easily to present them to you in their simplest forms. If you are one of those people like me who doesn't like eating breakfast in the morning, the smoothie recipes in this book will do the trick for you.

1 or 2 cups of your favorite smoothie will work as a great replacement of breakfast and load you with energy that will help you go through the day easily without feeling tired often like you are used to. All the ingredients in the following smoothies are healthy and packed with benefits, so you won't ever feel guilty for eating something as tasty as that.

If you have kids, or you know someone who doesn't like eating veggies and fruits, these recipes are the ultimate gift that you can ever offer them because you will get them to eat healthier and tastier food at the same time.

If you are going to the gym, work or on a trip and you want something to keep you full and work as a great replacement of coffee, an amazing smoothie is all that you need. Unlike coffee that will cause you to stress and become addicted to it, a different smoothie every day will keep your body full of energy, and you won't cause you any side effect!!

Eat healthy and enjoy.

Anti-Aging Cacao Dates
(ready in about 2 minutes | Servings 2)

Ingredients:

- 6 dates, pitted
- ½ cup of coconut milk
- ¼ cup of cacao powder
- 2 tablespoons of sweetener
- 2 cups of low fat milk
- 6 ice cubes

Directions:

1. Combine all the ingredients in your Ninja Blender and blend them on high speed for 45 sec.
2. Once the time is up, serve it right away and enjoy.

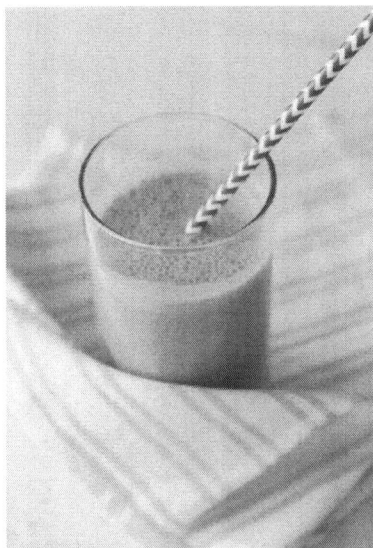

Anti-Aging Chocolaty Tofu

(ready in about 2 minutes | Servings 2)

Ingredients:

- ½ cup of cacao syrup
- 2 cups of boiling water
- 6 ice cubes
- 1 cup of silken tofu
- 1 cup of dates
- ½ cup of almonds

Directions:

1. Combine the boiling water with cacao syrup, dates and almonds in your Ninja Blender and allow them to sit for 10 min.

2. Once the time is up, stir in the tofu with ice and blend them on high speed for 45 sec then serve it right away and enjoy.

Athletic Performance Honey Pineapple Smoothie

(ready in about 2 minutes | Servings 2)

Ingredients:

- 1 ½ cup of almond milk
- 1 cup of pineapple, diced
- 1 ½ cups of coconut water
- ¼ cup of coconut flesh, shredded
- ½ teaspoon of vanilla extract
- 2 tablespoons of honey

Directions:

1. Combine all the ingredients in your Ninja Blender and blend them on high speed for 45 sec.
2. Once the time is up, serve it right away and enjoy.

Athletic Performance Peanut Banana Smoothie

(ready in about 2 minutes | Servings 2)

Ingredients:

- 1 ½ banana
- 6 strawberries
- 1 cup of plain yogurt
- 1 ½ cups of low fat milk
- ¼ cup of peanut butter
- The flesh of 1 honeydew
- 1 tablespoon of flax seed oil

Directions:

1. Combine all the ingredients in your Ninja Blender and blend them on high speed for 45 sec.
2. Once the time is up, serve it right away and enjoy.

Honeydew Beauty Tea

(ready in about 2 minutes | Servings 2)

Ingredients:

- 1 ½ cups of brewed green tea
- 1 honeydew
- ½ cup of low fat milk
- 2 tablespoons of honey
- 1 ½ bananas

Directions:

1. Combine all the ingredients in your Ninja Blender and blend them on high speed for 45 sec.
2. Once the time is up, serve it right away and enjoy.

Healthy Hair Coconut Kale Smoothie

(ready in about 2 minutes | Servings 2)

Ingredients:

- 2 cups kale, finely chopped
- ¼ cup of honey
- 1 ½ banana
- 6 ice cubes
- 2 tablespoon flaxseed oil
- ½ teaspoon of coconut extract
- 6 ice cubes

Directions:

1. Combine all the ingredients in your Ninja Blender and blend them on high speed for 45 sec.
2. Once the time is up, serve it right away and enjoy.

Healthy Skin Strawberries Lemon

(ready in about 2 minutes | Servings 2)

Ingredients:

- 1 cup of strawberries
- 2 cups of low fat milk
- ¼ cup of lemon juice
- 6 ice cubes
- 1 teaspoon of lemon zest
- 10 almonds

Directions:

1. Combine all the ingredients in your Ninja Blender and blend them on high speed for 45 sec.
2. Once the time is up, serve it right away and enjoy.

Beauty Minty Chocolate Oats

(ready in about 2 minutes | Servings 2)

Ingredients:

- ½ cup of dry oats
- 2 cups of low fat milk
- ½ cup of chocolate protein powder
- 2 cups of spinach, frozen
- ½ teaspoon of peppermint extract
- ½ cup of fry oats

Directions:

1. Combine all the ingredients in your Ninja Blender and blend them on high speed for 45 sec.
2. Once the time is up, serve it right away and enjoy.

Bones and Joints Vanilla Jam
(ready in about 2 minutes | Servings 2)

Ingredients:
- ¼ cup of any jam
- 6 ice cubes
- ¼ cup of low fat yogurt
- 2 ½ cup of low fat milk
- ¼ cup of peanut butter
- ½ teaspoon of vanilla

Directions:

1. Combine all the ingredients in your Ninja Blender and blend them on high speed for 45 sec.
2. Once the time is up, serve it right away and enjoy.

Detoxification Cinnamon Raisins Smoothie

(ready in about 2 minutes | Servings 2)

Ingredients:

- 6 ice cubes
- 1 ½ cups of low fat milk
- ¼ cup of raisins
- 1 tablespoon of honey
- 2 teaspoons of cinnamon
- 1 cup of low fat vanilla yogurt

Directions:

1. Combine all the ingredients in your Ninja Blender and blend them on high speed for 45 sec.
2. Once the time is up, serve it right away and enjoy.

Detoxification Sunday Smoothie

(ready in about 2 minutes | Servings 2)

Ingredients:

- 1 ½ cups of chocolate milk
- 1 ½ cups of strawberries
- ½ cup of chocolate protein powder
- 2 teaspoons of ground flaxseed
- 1 cup of vanilla yogurt

Directions:

1. Combine all the ingredients in your Ninja Blender and blend them on high speed for 45 sec.
2. Once the time is up, serve it right away and enjoy.

Blood Sugar Control Chocolate Banana Butter

(ready in about 2 minutes | Servings 2)

Ingredients:

- 6 ice cubes
- 3 tablespoon sweetener
- 2 cups of low fat chocolate milk
- 1 ½ bananas
- ¼ cup of peanut butter

Directions:

1. Combine all the ingredients in your Ninja Blender and blend them on high speed for 45 sec.
2. Once the time is up, serve it right away and enjoy.

Energy Beachy Berries

(ready in about 2 minutes | Servings 2)

Ingredients:

- 1 ½ cups of strawberries
- ¼ cup of chia seeds
- 1 ½ bananas
- 2 tablespoons of honey
- 2 cups of low fat milk

Directions:

1. Combine all the ingredients in your Ninja Blender and blend them on high speed for 45 sec.
2. Once the time is up, serve it right away and enjoy.

Heart Health Spicy Avocado

(ready in about 2 minutes | Servings 2)

Ingredients:

- 1 dash of cayenne pepper
- 14 ounces of carrot juice
- 1 cup of avocado
- 6 ice cubes
- 1 ½ tablespoons of fresh ginger, sliced
- ¼ cup of lemon juice

Directions:

1. Combine all the ingredients in your Ninja Blender and blend them on high speed for 45 sec.
2. Once the time is up, serve it right away and enjoy.

Detoxification Watermelon
(ready in about 2 minutes | Servings 2)

Ingredients:

- 1 medium sized watermelon, seedless and cut into chunks
- 6 ice cubes
- ½ cup of low fat milk
- 1 cup of low fat yogurt
- ¼ cup of protein powder
- 1 cup of strawberries

Directions:

1. Combine all the ingredients in your Ninja Blender and blend them on high speed for 45 sec.
2. Once the time is up, serve it right away and enjoy.

Immune Boosting Green Spring Berries
(ready in about 2 minutes | Servings2)

Ingredients:

- 1 tablespoon of flaxseed
- ½ cup of mixed berries
- 1 banana
- 1 orange, sliced
- ½ avocado
- 1 cup of spring water

Directions:

1. Combine all the ingredients in your Ninja Blender and blend them on high speed for 45 sec.
2. Once the time is up, serve it right away and enjoy.

Immune Boosting Smooth Green Apples

(ready in about 2 minutes | Servings 2)

Ingredients:

- 1 tablespoon of psyllium husks
- 1 apple, sliced
- 1 tablespoon of lime juice
- 2 tablespoon of lemon juice
- ½ cup of parsley, chopped
- 1 stalk of celery stalk, finely chopped
- 1 cup of kale, finely chopped
- 1 cup of cucumber, finely chopped

Directions:

1. Combine all the ingredients in your Ninja Blender and blend them on high speed for 45 sec.
2. Once the time is up, serve it right away and enjoy.

Kid-Friendly Pomegranate Summer

(ready in about 2 minutes | Servings 2)

Ingredients:

- ½ cup of ice cubes
- 6 strawberries
- ½ banana
- 1 cup of plain yogurt
- 1 cup of pomegranate juice

Directions:

1. Combine all the ingredients in your Ninja Blender and blend them on high speed for 45 sec.
2. Once the time is up, serve it right away and enjoy.

Kid-Friendly Blackberries Milk
(ready in about 2 minutes | Servings 2)

Ingredients:

- ½ cup of soy milk
- ½ cup of spring water
- 1 cup of plain yogurt
- ¼ cup of rolled oats
- ½ cup of blackberries
- ¼ cup of soy milk

Directions:

1. Combine all the ingredients in your Ninja Blender and blend them on high speed for 45 sec.
2. Once the time is up, serve it right away and enjoy.

Mood-Enhancing Greek Honey Banana

(ready in about 2 minutes | Servings 2)

Ingredients:

- 1 cup of soy milk
- ¼ cup of Greek yogurt
- 1 cup of kale
- ½ cup of ice cubes
- ¼ cup of blueberries
- 1 tablespoon of flaxseed
- 3 tablespoons of honey
- 1 banana

Directions:

1. Combine all the ingredients in your Ninja Blender and blend them on high speed for 45 sec.
2. Once the time is up, serve it right away and enjoy.

Anti-Aging Swiss Spring Berries
(ready in about 2 minutes | Servings 2)

Ingredients:

- 1 banana, sliced
- 1 cup of swiss chard
- ½ cup of blueberries
- 1 cup of spring water
- ½ cup of ice cubes
- 1 teaspoon of fresh finger, sliced
- 1 banana

Directions:

1. Combine all the ingredients in your Ninja Blender and blend them on high speed for 45 sec.
2. Once the time is up, serve it right away and enjoy.

Anti – Stress Strawberry Oatmeal

(ready in about 2 minutes | Servings 2)

Ingredients:

- 1 cup of almond milk
- ½ cup of strawberries
- 1 banana
- ½ cup of rolled oats

Directions:

1. Combine all the ingredients in your Ninja Blender and blend them on high speed for 45 sec.
2. Once the time is up, serve it right away and enjoy.

Weight Loss Peanut Tofu Smoothie

(ready in about 2 minutes | Servings 2)

Ingredients:

- 4 tablespoons of peanut butter
- ½ cup of milk
- 1 banana, frozen
- ½ cup of tofu
- Honey

Directions:

1. Combine all the ingredients in your Ninja Blender and blend them on high speed for 45 sec.
2. Once the time is up, serve it right away and enjoy.

Fat Burning Peanut Banana

(ready in about 2 minutes | Servings 2)

Ingredients:

- 2 tablespoons of peanut butter
- ½ cup of ice cubes
- ½ cup of mixed berries
- 1 banana
- 2 tablespoons of honey
- ½ cup of almond milk

Directions:

1. Combine all the ingredients in your Ninja Blender and blend them on high speed for 45 sec.
2. Once the time is up, serve it right away and enjoy.

The Complete Meal Coconut Grapefruit

(ready in about 2 minutes | Servings 2)

Ingredients:

- 1 banana
- 2 tablespoons of coconut oil
- 1 cup of spring water
- ½ cup of ice cubes
- 2 tablespoons of honey
- 1 cup of kale

Directions:

1. Combine all the ingredients in your Ninja Blender and blend them on high speed for 45 sec.

2. Once the time is up, serve it right away and enjoy.

Energy Pineapple Minty Fennel

(ready in about 2 minutes | Servings 2)

Ingredients:

- ½ ounce of mint, finely chopped
- ½ cup of pineapple chunks
- 1 cup of spring water
- ½ cup of ice cubes
- ½ cup of fennel, finely chopped
- ½ avocado, sliced

Directions:

1. Combine all the ingredients in your Ninja Blender and blend them on high speed for 45 sec.
2. Once the time is up, serve it right away and enjoy.

Sweet Vanilla Apple Pie

(ready in about 2 minutes | Servings 2)

Ingredients:

- 8 ice cubes
- 4 tablespoons of cashews butter
- 8 ice cubes
- 2 teaspoons of apple pie spice
- 2 apples, sliced
- 12 ounces of vanilla yogurt
- 1 cup of low fat vanilla yogurt

Directions:

1. Combine all the ingredients in your Ninja Blender and blend them on high speed for 45 sec.
2. Once the time is up, serve it right away and enjoy.

Clean Orangey Mixed Berries Smoothie

(ready in about 2 minutes | Servings 2)

Ingredients:

- 2 tablespoons of sweetener
- 1 ½ cups of orange juice
- 2 avocadoes
- ¾ cup of raspberries, frozen
- 1 ½ cups of strawberry juice

Directions:

1. Combine all the ingredients in your Ninja Blender and blend them on high speed for 45 sec.
2. Once the time is up, serve it right away and enjoy.

Detoxification Swiss Lemon Smoothie

(ready in about 2 minutes | Servings 2)

Ingredients:

- 2 tablespoons of lemon juice
- 1 tablespoon of ground flaxseed
- ½ avocado, sliced
- ½ cup of ice cubes
- ½ cup of soy milk
- 1 cup of Swiss chard
- 1 banana
- ¼ cup of fresh mint, finely chopped
- 1 cup of spring water

Directions:

1. Combine all the ingredients in your Ninja Blender and blend them on high speed for 45 sec.

2. Once the time is up, serve it right away and enjoy

No Constipation Chocolate Banana Split

(ready in about 2 minutes | Servings 2)

Ingredients:

- ¾ cup of silken tofu
- 3 tablespoons of honey
- ¼ cup of cacao powder
- 1 ½ bananas
- 1 ½ cups of low fat milk

Directions:

1. Combine all the ingredients in your Ninja Blender and blend them on high speed for 30 to 45 sec.
2. Once the time is up, serve it right away and enjoy

Fat Burning Peanut Banana Smoothie

(ready in about 2 minutes | Servings 2)

Ingredients:

- 8 ice cubes
- 2 tablespoons of protein powder
- 1 banana
- 1 ¼ cup of low fat milk
- 2/3 cup of peanut butter

Directions:

1. Combine all the ingredients in your Ninja Blender and blend them on high speed until they become smooth and creamy then serve it right away and enjoy.

No Diabetes Classic Vanilla Berries

(ready in about 2 minutes | Servings 2)

Ingredients:

- 1 tablespoon of sweetener
- ½ banana
- 1 ½ cup of mixed berries, frozen
- 6 ice cubes
- 1 ½ cups of vanilla yogurt

Directions:

1. Combine all the ingredients in your Ninja Blender and blend them on high speed for 45 sec.
2. Once the time is up, serve it right away and enjoy.

Glowing Skin Blue Honey Smoothie
(ready in about 2 minutes | Servings 2)

Ingredients:

- 6 ice cubes
- 16 ounces of water
- ½ cup of blueberries, frozen
- 1 banana
- 2/3 cup of soy protein powder
- 1 tablespoon of flaxseed oil

Directions:

1. Combine all the ingredients in your Ninja Blender and blend them on high speed for 45 sec.
2. Once the time is up, serve it right away and enjoy.

Victoria's Secret Body Cashew Yogurt

(ready in about 2 minutes | Servings 2)

Ingredients:

- 1 tablespoon of flaxseed oil
- 3 tablespoons of sweetener
- 1 tablespoon of vanilla extract
- 1 ½ banana
- 2 tablespoons of cashews butter
- 1 cup of low fat yogurt

Directions:

1. Combine all the ingredients in your Ninja Blender and blend them on high speed for 45 sec.
2. Once the time is up, serve it right away and enjoy.

Mood-Enhancing Citrus Orange

(ready in about 2 minutes | Servings 2)

Ingredients:

- 2 oranges, sliced
- 1 ½ cups of soy milk
- 8 ice cubes
- 1 ½ tablespoon of flaxseed oil
- 12 ounces of citrus yogurt

Directions:

1. Combine all the ingredients in your Ninja Blender and blend them on high speed for 45 sec.
2. Once the time is up, serve it right away and enjoy.

Healthy Eyes Honey Oranges
(ready in about 2 minutes | Servings 2)

Ingredients:

- 8 ice cubes
- 1 ½ orange, sliced
- ½ cup of apple, sliced
- 1 banana
- 3 tablespoons of honey
- 1 cup of low fat milk

Directions:

1. Combine all the ingredients in your Ninja Blender and blend them on high speed for 45 sec.
2. Once the time is up, serve it right away and enjoy.

Amazing Hair Classic Tropical Pineapple

(ready in about 8 hours 15 minutes | Servings 6)

Ingredients:

- 3 tablespoons of sweetener
- 8 ounces of pineapple chunks
- 1 ½ cups of low fat milk
- 2 tablespoons of flaxseed oil
- 1 ½ cups of low fat milk

Directions:

1. Combine all the ingredients in your Ninja Blender and blend them on high speed for 45 sec.
2. Once the time is up, serve it right away and enjoy.

Anti-Aging Hot Summery Tomato
(ready in about 2 minutes | Servings 2)

Ingredients:

- 9 ice cubes
- 2/3 cup of celery, finely chopped
- 1 ½ cups of tomato, chopped
- 1 cup of tomato juice
- ½ cup of apple juice
- 2/3 teaspoon of hot sauce
- 23 cup of carrots, finely chopped

Directions:

1. Combine all the ingredients in your Ninja Blender and blend them on high speed for 45 sec.

2. Once the time is up, serve it right away and enjoy.

Detoxification Green Ginger Smoothie

(ready in about 2 minutes | Servings 1)

Ingredients:

- 1 cup of kale
- 1 apple, cored and sliced
- 1 cup of spring water
- ½ lemon, sliced
- 1 stalk of celery, chopped
- ½ cucumber, chopped
- ¼ bunch of parsley, chopped
- 2 teaspoons of fresh ginger, sliced

Directions:

1. Combine all the ingredients in your Ninja Blender and blend them on high speed for 45 sec.

2. Once the time is up, serve it right away and enjoy.

Kid-Friendly Pink Lime Smoothie

(ready in 2 minutes | Servings 2)

Ingredients:

- 1 ½ cup of lime sherbet
- 8 ice cubes
- ¾ cup of lime, sliced
- 2/3 cup of strawberries
- 1 ½ cup of low fat milk

Directions:

1. Combine all the ingredients in your Ninja Blender and blend them on high speed for 45 sec.
2. Once the time is up, serve it right away and enjoy.

Glowing Skin Vanilla Mango Bliss

(ready in about 2 minutes | Servings 2)

Ingredients:

- ½ cup of mango chunks
- 5 ice cubes
- 1 cup of mango juice
- 2 tablespoons of sweetener
- 2 tablespoons of lime juice
- ½ cup of vanilla low fat yogurt
- ½ avocado

Directions:

1. Combine all the ingredients in your Ninja Blender and blend them on high speed until you are satisfied then serve your smoothie right away and enjoy.

No Stress Cantaloupe Raspberries Smoothie

(ready in about 2 minutes | Servings 2)

Ingredients:

- 8 ice cubes
- 3 cup of cantaloupe chunks
- 1 ½ cups of lettuce, chopped
- 1 ½ cup of raspberries
- 8 ice cubes

Directions:

1. Combine all the ingredients in your Ninja Blender and blend them on high speed for 45 sec.
2. Once the time is up, serve it right away and enjoy.

Energy Vanilla Espresso

(ready in about 2 minutes | Servings 2)

Ingredients:

- 6 ice cubes
- 2 shots of espresso
- 4 teaspoons of cacao powder
- 1 cup of low fat vanilla yogurt
- 2 tablespoons of chia seeds
- 2 tablespoons of sweetener

Directions:

1. Combine all the ingredients in your Ninja Blender and blend them on high speed for 45 sec.

2. Once the time is up, serve it right away and enjoy.

Beach Body Soft Peach

(ready in about 2 | Servings 2)

Ingredients:

- 1 ½ cups of low fat milk
- 3 tablespoons of sweetener
- 1 ½ cups of peaches, sliced and frozen
- 1 tablespoon of chia seeds
- 4 ice cubes

Directions:

1. Combine all the ingredients in your Ninja Blender and blend them on high speed for 45 sec.
2. Once the time is up, serve it right away and enjoy.

Weight Loss Chocolaty Raspberries

(ready in about 2 minutes | Servings 2)

Ingredients:

- 1 ½ cups of raspberries juice
- 6 ice cubes
- 1 cup of low fat milk
- 10 ounces of vanilla yogurt
- ½ cup of dark chocolate chips

Directions:

1. Combine all the ingredients in your Ninja Blender and blend them on high speed for 45 sec.
2. Once the time is up, serve it right away and enjoy.

Anti-Aging Creamy Pink Banana Smoothie
(ready in about 2 minutes | Servings 2)

Ingredients:

- 1 cup of low fat vanilla yogurt
- 1 ½ cups of strawberries
- 6 ice cubes
- ½ up of orange juice
- 1 ½ banana
- 1 orange, sliced

Directions:

1. Combine all the ingredients in your Ninja Blender and blend them on high speed for 45 sec.
2. Once the time is up, serve it right away and enjoy.

Immune Boosting Spinach Strawberries

(ready in about 2 minutes | Servings 2)

Ingredients:

- ¼ cup of orange juice
- 6 ounces of plain yogurt
- 4 baby carrots
- 1 tablespoon of dry oat meal
- 1 teaspoon of flaxseed oil
- ½ cup of spinach
- ¼ cup of protein powder
- ½ banana
- ¼ cup of strawberries
- 4 ice cubes

Directions:

1. Combine all the ingredients in your Ninja Blender and blend them on high speed for 45 sec.
2. Once the time is up, serve it right away and enjoy.

Antioxidant Booster Fruity Protein Smoothie

(ready in about 2 minutes | Servings 2)

Ingredients:

- ½ cup of low fat milk
- 2 bananas, frozen
- 1 ½ cups of peaches, sliced and frozen
- ½ cup of blueberries
- 2 tablespoons of protein powder
- 1 cup of low fat yogurt

Directions:

1. Combine all the ingredients in your Ninja Blender and blend them on high speed for 45 sec.
2. Once the time is up, serve it right away and enjoy

Tropical Island Basic Mango Smoothie

(ready in about 2 minutes | Servings 2)

Ingredients:

- 1 mango, chopped
- ½ cup of ice cubes
- ½ banana
- 1 cup of soy milk

Directions:

1. Combine all the ingredients in your Ninja Blender and blend them on high speed for 45 sec.
2. Once the time is up, serve it right away and enjoy.

Heart Health Peanut and Vanilla Ice Cream

(ready in about 2 minutes | Servings 2)

Ingredients:

- ½ cup of ice cubes
- 1 cup of almond milk
- ½ cup of vanilla ice cream
- ¼ cup of peanut butter

Directions:

1. Combine all the ingredients in your Ninja Blender and blend them on high speed for 30 to 45 sec.
2. Once the time is up, serve it right away and enjoy.

Your Free Gift

I wanted to show my appreciation that you support my work so I've put together a free gift for you.

Slowcooker Essentials Cookbook
http://thezenfactory.com/ninja_master_free_book/

Just visit the link above to download it now.

I know you will love this gift.

Thanks!

Conclusion

Thank you again for downloading this book! I really do hope you found the recipes as tasty and mouth watering as I did.

Thank You

Printed in Great Britain
by Amazon